I0839059

Don't Wash Your Net Yet

The Reward of Not Giving Up

Chidi ObiGod

Kisswriters

Copyright © 2020 Chidi ObiGod

All rights reserved

The characters and events portrayed in this book are fictitious. Any similarity to real persons, living or dead, is coincidental and not intended by the author.

No part of this book may be reproduced, or stored in a retrieval system, or transmitted in any form or by any means, electronic, mechanical, photocopying, recording, or otherwise, without express written permission of the publisher.

This book is dedicated to suicidal friend of mine.

Contents

ACKNOWLEDGE-MENT

All glory returns to the Almighty God who has never given up on me despite how many times I have tried giving up on myself.

Special thanks to my mother Elizabeth ObiGod, who never for once allowed me to watch my net. Mum, you are a beautiful rock in my life.

Thanks to wonderful friend Chinenye Ubah, you always stand by me and give me reasons to hold on.

INTRODUCTION

One cool afternoon, I decided to sit back and watch a movie that a friend of mine gave me. It was a Hollywood movie titled The Two Pope which tells the story of Cardinal Joseph Ratzinger who later became Pope Benedict XVI and Cardinal Jorge Bergoglio who came to the Pope because he wanted to resign from his position as a cardinal archbishop. Cardinal Bergoglio believed that the Roman Catholic Church needed a reformation which was not coming forth. He was tired of his position and he thought he has come to the climax of it that he couldn't continue. There was nothing he was looking forward to again. He thought that the best thing was for him to wash his net and quit. So he came to the Pope to sign his resignation letter.

His meeting with the pope started with them trying to settle their theological differences. Later they retired to Papacy's residential house. After dinner, they sat down to know each other better. To his greatest surprise, he found out that the Pope was having his own challenges and pressure. The Pope opened up to him about the challenges of the papacy. My best part of the movie is this part of their conversation.

The Pope: *You know the hardest thing is to listen to hear His voice. Gods voice.*

Cardinal Bergoglio: *Sorry, even for a pope?*

The Pope: *But perhaps especially for the pope. (He coughed). You know, when I was a young man, some years ago, I always knew what He wanted of me. What God wanted, what purpose He has for me. But* *now… Perhaps I need to listen more intently. Perhaps, I need a spiritual hearing aid. Who does* know*?*

Cardinal Bergoglio came to resign and wash his net as Gods fisherman but he didn't know that God had a better plan for him as he later succeeded Pope Benedict XIV to become the present Pope Francis. Pope Benedict XIV resigned from the office which shocked the entire world on February 28 of 2013. He did so because he came to that point that he didn't know what more God had for him. The pressure was too high, his health was not helping matters and he resigned from the greatest office of Roman Catholic Christianity.

I know you are not a pope to relate to this but the pope is a human like you and he has personal and professional challenges just like you. You may see the pope as the holiest person on earth yet that didn't exempt him from the challenges of life. He prayed and he felted God wasn't answering him, at a point he felt God wasn't talking to him anymore. If challenges could make a pope quit his exalted office, don't think that the reason for your present predicament is because you are a terrible sinner who to make confessions and things will become perfect.

If you have a very big destiny you must understand that your challenges may be big as well. Even if you are religious and righteous it will not exempt you from the test of life. Sometimes you will not get to have what you want when you want it. Sometimes life can be very disappointing that you will look back at your life and think you have wasted your life doing the right thing.

Those two men were ordinary human beings before they become popes. And as an ordinary person you are, you don't know what the future holds for you. Before you wear the crown of glory in life, you must live through a bizarre story that will serve as experiences that will prepare you for greatness.

Roman Catholic Church believes that the pope sits on the throne of Saint Peter who they claim is the first pope. St. Peter was like the assistant of our Lord Jesus Christ when he was alive. He was among the three inner circles of Jesus discipline that he followed Jesus everywhere he went. Even when Jesus died, St. Peter was the one that led the ancient church. He was the first to take the gospel to the gentiles and got them filled with Holy Spirit. He was a strong pillar of the early church if not the strongest pillar.

Peter in his greatness didn't smoothly start his journey to glory. He started as Simon the local fisherman in Gennesaret. He had moments that he wanted to quit just like me and you. He had moments of failures, disappointments, and frustrations. He had moments when things were rough and life made no sense. He had moments when he saw no reasons to live yet something remarkable happened in his life that brought transformation.

If you are passing through a lot in life that you want to give up, this book is for you. If you think you have no reason to go on in life or hold on in pursuing whatever you want to achieve this book is for you.

CHAPTER 1.

THE GROPING GREAT

And it came to pass, that, as the people pressed upon him to hear the word of God, he stood by the lake of Gennesaret, and saw two ships standing by the lake: but the fishermen were gone out of them, and were washing their nets. (Luke 5:1-2)

The office of God is the busiest office ever known, located in the fiery mountain far in the northern side of the heaven in the unapproachable light. His all-seeing eyes run to and fro faster than any satellite ever seen that nothing escapes his sight, even the beds of hell, the heart of darkness, the uttermost parts of the sea all lay bare before him. Every second of the day billions of prayers pop into his ears, his desk is fully loaded with uncountable files of cases to be settled. And his hands are constantly doing wonders and working miracles. He is responsible for feeding the cattle upon a thousand hills, the innumerable beasts of the field that look up to him to get their daily foods, yet his eyes are still upon the little sparrows to satisfy them. And when he opens his mouth to speak billions upon billions of creatures open their hungry ear to listen to him.

The fact that God is a specialist in impossibilities and the Chief consultant in problems that are considered unsolvable makes billions of people press on him for the solution on a second basis. Jesus was God in the flesh who came as fresh air to millions that are being suffocated by the problems of life. When wine finished in a wedding in Cana in Galilee Jesus was the One they called upon to save the day. When a child died in her sleep out of fever it was Jesus that was called to tell her *Talitha Cumi*. The sick pressed on him to get healed, the weak pressed on him to be strengthened, the hungry pressed on him to be fed. What amazes me is that some people even take from him without his permission like the woman with issues of blood that came from behind and took virtue from him without his permission and he never complained because He is the fountain of life forever oozing and never runs dry.

Then in the midst of all these, he still has time for people who have no time for him. He sends rain upon the just and unjust, his eyes still see the opportunity to bless them, and his hand quick to reach out and help them. No matter how busy you think God is, your matter is not trivia to him.

Jesus had multitudes listening to him in his city-wide crusade yet something crucial caught his attention. It was the picture of fishermen washing their net in frustration and it was also the picture of a business closing down because its owners have put a conclusion where he the Alpha and Omega is trying to make an introduction.

In the same way, he sees the picture of failing marriages because the couples have concluded that it is not working. He sees a young man who wants to take his own life because he thinks there's no more good reason to live. He sees a young woman who wants to give up on love because she somehow believes love is not for her, all men are the same, and they come to hurt her not to love her. He sees people who put a full stop when he has placed a comma.

The bible stated that Jesus demanded Simon's ship and entered into the ship to use it for divine purposes. Nothing happens by chance, that you bought or picked up this book to read, or someone gave it to you is because Jesus has decided to enter your ship and turn things around. You may wonder why God will choose someone like you because you consider yourself as a non-entity but what you don't know is there's something about you that meets the eyes of the Almighty and He will not allow you to give up on a great destiny that is ahead of you.

IN YOUR EYES

I am sure the man named Simon used to see himself as nothing more than a local fisherman. His father was a fisherman, he was born into the business and inherited his father's skills, boat, and merchandise, he grew up among other fishermen and definitely he never saw his life beyond the lake of Gennesaret.

You may blame him for not attending the crusade where Jesus was preaching and teaching people the word of God that would change their story, but he had no reason to do that. He had heard about Jesus the young orator and miracle worker before, people spoke so much and highly of him, he heard he was someone men should reckon with, someone people run to in the time of need. Yet Simon had a way of excusing himself from such things, he didn't think he had free time like people who were listening to Jesus, he considered them to be elites who seek a special kind of knowledge or a group of simpletons who were being brainwashed. And he didn't belong to any of them.

He told himself that those crowds listening to Jesus must be well fed to spare some time to go and listen to a young orator, and such stupidity was not for a young man like him with a lot of responsibilities and mouths to feed. He would have considered attending the crusade on a good day but not today which was worse than the worst of days. He had just rebuked a fellow fisherman who greeted him Good morning, a few minutes ago that there was nothing good about the morning. How would he go back home empty-handed to face his expectant wife and his hungry children who would not hesitate to ask him, Daddy, what did you catch today?

Frustration covered his face like snows cover Mount Everest, the fear of being seen as a failure was eating up his gut as a fluke worm. He didn't want to prove his haters right. He had lived his life trying to make his father the old fisherman proud. He remembered the face of his son who always looked up to him as his role model. The last time a similar thing happened he gave his wife excuses but no more excuses to give this time around. For the first time in his fishing life, Simon felt he was a failure.

What we are passing through in life and what we went through in the past have a way of defining us to ourselves. You can easily see yourself as a mess because you have messed up in a lot of things. You can tag yourself as a failure in your mind because you have failed times without numbers in different things. In your eyes, you are good for nothing fellow because you have tried different things that you are not good at. The circumstances of life can lie to you about your true identity and it can remain your reality as long as you live in ignorance of who you are.

If you could see yourself in terms of your true potential, you may not recognize yourself. If you were to see yourself as you could be, you will marvel at the fact that you are selling yourself short.

There's a story about a man who died and went to heaven. While strolling the golden street of heaven he met one of the wise elders of heaven. The man stopped the wise elder and enquired from him, Holy One, while on earth I had an interest in the military. That I was wondering who the greatest General of all time was. Please can you help and tell me who it was?

The wise elder replied, "Oh, that's not a hard question. It's that man over there." He pointed at a man sitting at yonder.

"Wait! That man over there? You must be mistaken," responded the man as he couldn't believe his eyes. "I know that man on earth and he was just a common laborer."

"That's right," assured the wise elder. "He would have been

the greatest General of all time if he had been a General."

The man was the greatest general of all time but he groped his way through life and the best he could do was to be a common laborer because he didn't know who he was.

To me, Saint Peter is the greatest apostle of all time but he could have lived and died a fisherman. Do you know how many greatest of all times men and women walking hopelessly in our street? They just don't know who they are.

IN THE EYES OF PEOPLE

I am sure many people in that town of Gennesaret don't know the true name of Simon; they know him as the Fisherman. They defined him by his profession, career, and business. They defined him by how fast his business was growing, how big his boat was, how many ships he had, how large was his net and they determined his net worth by how many catches he made in a day and how he networked his sales.

On that hazy morning, Simon was not only disappointed with himself that he made no catch, he felt that he disappointed a lot of people especially the ones who depended on him for their supply of fish. He felt he disappointed his customers, his business partners, his brand loyalists. Being a fisherman was what made him relevant, it was what defined him and he couldn't afford to lose that.

People don't seem to care about who you are, they care more about the services you lender to them. They don't know your name because they know you by the product you sell or the services you provide. They know you as the doctor or nurse who treats them when they are sick. The hairstylist by the street who fixes their hair. The lawyer who handles their legal cases. The salesperson who supplies them with this and that. That bus driver. The preacher. That plumber. The school teacher. The real estate lady. What you do is what defines you in their eyes.

In the eyes of people, you are relevant as long as you are

successful and progressing. Success brings relevance. And success becomes a serious pressure because you don't want to lose relevance. None of us wants to disappoint people who depend on us for something. You don't want to disappoint your clients, customers, employers, fans, and followers. Don't be fooled to believe you are friends with some people; they stick around you because when they need fish you provide it, they are not your friends of love but out of convenience. So to remain a successful fisherman in their eyes you do everything possible to maintain the supply of fishes.

You don't want to lose your job, career, or relationship not because it is not working but because to you that's what gives you relevance. So to remain in the job, you do everything possible because to you the job defines you. You do what you are not comfortable with within a relationship to stay in the relationship because to you that's what defines you. So many people do a lot of crazy things these days to get attention, to get followers on social media, and to become famous because to them that is what defines them. Seeing yourself from the eyes of others can be a road to frustration in disguise. Just ask some celebrities they will tell you better.

Celebrities don't understand how people will meet them and in a space of five minutes they ask for an autograph and pose for a photograph, then they walk away with a picture just to show their friends I know this famous person. They know nothing.

The truth is this - nobody really knows you, most people don't want to know you, they only want to be recognized with you especially if you are famous. They won't benefit from you and what you have something to offer. So they have no right to define you because they don't know you, as much as they claim they do you know they don't know you.

I know you don't want to be defined by your circumstances, your flaws, and your mistakes. You don't want anyone to put a negative tag on you that it takes over your real name like we see in the Bible where a man was called Blind Bartimaeus and a certain woman was called the woman with the issue of blood - which their ailment took over their name. For that reason, you created a mask for yourself to avoid people putting a tag or label on you. You wear the mask in public and project the fake you on social media. You are so good at wearing that mask that you have become a mistress of disguise. People like you for your mask, they fall in love with your mask, and the mask has made you famous, but only you know that is not the real you.

If you are a public figure who always wears a mask to appear perfect in the eyes of people, that you Photoshop your personality, you crop out all flaws and failures in order to look picture perfect remember you can't hind behind that pretty mask forever because that's not who you are. They depend on you to provide them with the fish of entertainment, sports, knowledge, etc. and you depend on them for relevance, if the fish stops coming from you they will stop following, and if you depend on their praise to be happy, you will surely get depressed when their praise is less.

You know for sure you are not who people think you are and you are not what they say you are. You are who God says you are.

FROM GODS LENS

The moment Jesus paused in his preaching and looked up, he saw two ships anchored by the bank of Lake Gennesaret, and his spiritual instinct directed him to enter a particular ship, not by coincidence but by divine mandate, he was not seeing an empty old rugged ship, he was seeing a great destiny behind the ship. He saw the owner who was squatting by the corner, frustration written all over his weary face as hot sluggish sweat dripped from his beard as drops of rain from a licking roof.

Jesus shook his head in amazement because in his mind he was thinking, "How I wish this young man knows who he is?" Jesus was actually looking at one of the greatest apostles of Christianity (a rock upon which he would build his church). He was looking at the man privileged enough to witness his transfiguration, the first man to witness his empty tomb after resurrection, the only man who followed his command and walked on water. The man who would receive the Holy Spirit and use a few minute sermons to convert three thousand souls overnight, a man whose shadow would heal the sick and cast out demons. He was looking at a man that would be immortalized among the believers as St. Peter that after two thousand years his name will be mentioned whenever the gospel goes.

I guess Simon didn't know all these things about himself. And like the man who would have become the greatest general ever lived; he was a great man groping around and was selling himself short because he had no clue who he was.

When Jesus looks at you, he smiles in amazement and says, "How I wish this my son or daughter will discover who he or she is. The simple truth is that there is more to you than meets the eyes. There is something great, peculiar, and unique about you that you don't know yet. You are not the little you or the poor you or the loser you. A great destiny awaits you and it is far beyond what you can imagine. And you cannot see this until you begin to see yourself the way God sees you.

King David later in his life understood it was only God who was his Maker that knew him more than he knew himself that he wrote in **Psalm 139:1- 16**

"O LORD, thou hast searched me, and known me. Thou knowest my downsitting and mine uprising, thou understandest my thought afar off. Thou compassest my path and my lying down, and art acquainted with all my ways. For there is not a word in my tongue, but, lo, O LORD, thou knowset it altogether. Thou hast beset me behind and before and laid thine hand upon me. Such knowledge is too wonderful for me; it is high, I cannot attain unto it... For thou has possessed my reins: thou hast covered me in my mothers womb. I will praise thee; for I am fearfully and wonderfully made: marvellous are thy works; and that my soul knoweth right well. My substance was not hid from thee, when I was made in secret, and curiously wrought in the lowest parts of the

earth. Thine eyes did see my substance, yet being unperfect; and in thy book all members were written, which in continuance were fashioned, when as yet there was none of them."

I don't care how you see yourself but you have to start seeing yourself the same way God sees you. You may see yourself as an old barren woman like Sarah and there is a dark fear in your heart that a prettier younger Egyptian (worldly) girl would come and take your place in marriage yet in the eyes of God, you are the mother of many nations.

You may see yourself as a poor guy who threshes wheat by the winepress as Gideon but in the eyes of God, you are a mighty man of valor. Yes, you see yourself as a common cashier in a local grocery store, an uneducated janitor with a very low income but in the eyes of God, you are a CEO of one of the largest companies in the state.

You may see yourself as a run-away refugee like Moses, but God sees you as the greatest leader and emancipator of his chosen people. You can easily disqualify and discredit yourself as a school dropout, a quitter, someone who is physically, financially, socially, and academically incapacitated but God sees none of that when he looks at you.

You may see yourself as a bad boy because earlier on in your life you were ostracized off to the wild part of life by family and the society like David but God looks at you daily and see a great king, a great leader of your nation.

You may be like Leah who gave everything to love and for love yet she never got it back the way she gave it, she felt incapable of love, ugly, used, and not always good enough. Never did she know that out of her womb would come Levi the priest of the nation and Judah the one who forever holds the scepter.

Until you start seeing yourself the same way God sees you, you will grope your way through life. You will jump from one job to another, one business to another, one relationship to another searching for what you cannot get, fishing for things your net can't catch, and by the time you have exhausted your force, you will retire to one corner of indulgence tired without any aspiration, then you begin to plan on how to watch the net.

Before you bend over to wash your net and give up before you say there is nothing more for you here, do you know who you are? You are far more than what you think you are and you are not even what people say you are. If you don't know who you are you will be like a lion who grew up among goats and he ate grass like them, he bleated where he should have roared because he had a wrong perception of himself not until he went to drink from a pool and he saw a reflection of himself in the mirror of life.

Jesus is that Mirror of Life, why not come and see.

When Nathanael came close, he got a reflection and a revelation of himself.

Jesus saw Nathanael coming to him, and saith to him, Behold an Israelite indeed, in whom is no guile! Nathanael saith unto him, whence knowest thou me? Jesus answered and said unto him, Before that Philip called thee, when thou wast under the fig tree, I saw thee. **(John1:48)**

He saw you before you saw yourself. Why not see yourself from his eyes? It is time for you to change your perception of yourself and grasp Gods perception of you. It is when you look at God that you will get a reflection of yourself. He is that crystal stream of life, when you come to drink you will see a reflection of the true you.

Like Simon God has been waiting for you to look to him and get a reflection and revelation of yourself but he doesn't seem to get your attention. When you are in need it is easy for you to get on your knees in prayer just to get Gods attention, but you don't know how God has been trying to get your attention so that He will give you a reflection and revelation of yourself because he knows you are a groping great man or woman, you are not living the life He created you to live, living far below your capacity.

Unfortunately, you can't give him your attention because

you are very busy with business.

CHAPTER 2.

BUSY WITH BUSINESS

Busy bees in business
Life's a golden fleece
Money is the honey
Dirt your skirt and shirt
Mag your swag as a tag.

These days our streets are busier than a beehive. The streets of New York City, Tokyo, London, Shanghai, Moscow, Mumbai, Singapore, Dubai, Sao Paulo, Delhi, Lagos, Cairo, and many other cities around the world are full of people who work harder than ants and busier than bees. An alarm clock is already installed in their head that by 3 am they are awake and work till dusk. We take pride in being workaholic that many of us boast they sleep 3 hours a day but they seem to forget what the bible said in Psalm 127 vs 2:
"In vain you rise early and stay up late, toiling for food to eat – for he grants sleep to those he loves." (NIV)

Life has become a rat race for some of us. Every day we have goals, plans, and agendas that we set out to accomplish, if it is not private then it is corporate. We have targets to meet, distances to cover, places to go, and meetings to attend. Many of us have their life well figured out, their visions were well written that their entire life is well mapped out and strategically graphed in a way they want it to be. It goes like these:

I'll finish secondary school by 15

Get admission to study the course of my dream by 16.

Graduate out of the university by 20.

Get a nice job by 21.

Get married by 25.

I will be done having children by 30, focus on my career or business.

I will be a millionaire on or before 31. Etc.

Wow. What a wonderful life, well planned and articulated. And there's a tendency you will work your muscles out to achieve all those. Then frustration hits like cancer when you don't achieve it at the time you planned. Some people are not good planners but good competitors. They are very good at competing with their friends, classmates, siblings that they don't know when they stop living their own lives. You may think you are a failure because all your mates have gone to school and you are not. You think you are left behind because all your friends are married except you. When you compare yourself with your siblings you think you are a retard. You think all your school classmates are ahead of you in life. Each time you see them, you feel bitter because you think they are doing better. No wonder you are so determined and desperate to succeed that you've resolved to be taking the pills of motivation and excess work lifestyle.

Motivational speakers spur us to work very hard that which is the main secret of success and they are very good at giving us one-sided stories of people who worked hard and actualized their goals. They give us lists of people who never quitted despite all odds and they fulfilled their dreams. But life is like a coin, it has two sides. We don't get to hear the other side of the coin where one works hard but doesn't get to make it to the pinnacle of success. They refused to quit and they died at their spot while trying. Unfortunately, we don't get to hear those stories.

We get to hear of Sir Edmund Hillary who was the first man to climb Mount Everest and we don't get to hear much of George Mallory who tried in the year 1924 and died on the way up. We get to hear about the guy who came first and nothing about the guy who came second. We celebrate the best contestant and overlook the runner-up, so nobody wants to be the second guy, nobody wants the consolation prize. The pressure to succeed is too high. The heat to come out as the best has burned some people up. We think that if we get this, achieve this and become that then we will be happy. But I am sorry to break it to you -you will be disappointed that you have been chasing frivolities all this while.

FISHERS OF FRIVOLITIES

We can call Simon a mere fisherman without knowing we are just like him. We may not be on a river with hooks and nets but we are in our offices, stores, and streets fishing for different things. Some fish for money, contracts, jobs, attention, recognition, fame, love, fun, properties, power, etc. The truth is that we all fish for different things in this sea called life. I may not be fishing exactly the same thing as what you fish for. All of us have something that makes us wake in the morning, take our bath, and hit the streets with our hooks in search of something to satisfy our desires and hunger. Not everyone is fishing for money. Some have their net full of it, so they are out there fishing for something that doesn't make sense to you.

Every year students graduate from colleges and universities just to be released into society as fishers. In fact, our school system seems to be structured in such a way that it only certifies us to fish in specialized rivers. Meanwhile, as undergraduates fish for the degrees at the same time many graduates who have gotten their degrees are fishing for jobs. At the other side of the river are people with jobs throwing their hook for promotions, nice cars, and houses.

Some ladies are under pressure to get married because the sun is going down on their face, so they put their nubile body as half-naked bait in a hook and cast it out to attract men but they end up in the hook of men who are sport-fishing for sexy women to satisfy their lust.

Yearly millions migrate from one country to another because somehow they believe fishing is better on the other side of the river. Some have gone back to school, add more degrees and skills to the ones they already have, so that they will graduate from fishing with a hook to fishing with a net. They have upgraded their merchandise from a canoe level to a ship level. Should I talk about net-workers who network themselves to wealth by building human pyramids? But we are all fishers fishing for frivolities and things that will satisfy us temporally, yet permanently our soul and spirit starve yearning for something our minds can't define.

If a man cannot live by bread alone then most of these things we fish for are mere frivolities in the sight of God because He knows we get our priorities wrong. Jesus said in Matthew 6:25-32:

"Therefore I say unto you, Take no thought for your life, what ye shall eat or what ye shall drink; nor yet for your body, what ye shall put on. Is not the life, more than meat, and the body than raiment? Behold the fowls of the air: for they sow not, neither do they reap, nor gather into barns; yet your heavenly Father feedeth them. Are ye not much better than they? Which of you by taking thought can add one cubit unto his stature? And why take ye thought for raiment? Consider the lilies of the field, how they grow; they toil not, neither do they spin. And yet I say unto you, That even Solomon in all his glory was not arrayed like one of these. Wherefore, if God so clothes the grass of the field, which today is, and tomorrow is cast into the oven, shall he not much more clothe you, O ye of little faith? Therefore take no thought, saying, what shall we eat? Or what shall we drink? Or, where withal shall we be clothed? (For afterall these things do the Gentiles seek) for your heav-

enly Father knoweth that ye have need of all these things."

HUSTLE MUST PAY

We've come to believe that for us to have essential things of life like food, clothes, and shelter we must work our muscles out. Some of us have nicknamed themselves HUSTLERS and believe success comes from how tedious someone hustles and toils so they have adopted a mantra with a hashtag: #Hustlemustpay.

But God is saying to us, Hey Hustler! Consider the birds of the air that have no shop or store, they have no profession or vocation, they have no certificate or advocate. The only thing they do is to chirp, fly around and sing sweet melodies as happy kindergarten kids singing nursery rhymes yet they eat to their fill and don't die of hunger.

Another picture is the picture of the Lilies of the field that does nothing but stand in one place, dance to the rhythm of the wind as pantomime dames in a colored array all waving uniformly to the beauty of nature. These Lilies and flowers that beautify nature can't move about so they are forever connected to their source which is the earth, believing that they will get their resources from their source the earth and the same way Fishes get their sustenance from the sea which is their source.

God is saying that if He can take care of these creatures considered to be of lesser importance how much more we who are created in His image and likeness, who are privileged to be called the children of God. You know when other creatures, bright and beautiful, great and small look at us human, they wonder and ask God, What is a man that thou are mindful of him?

And any man today who is a groping great it is because he is disconnected from God who is His source, so he is struggling where he should be soaring, crying in an area where he should be flying high until he realizes that Jesus is by the side trying to get his attention.

It was hard for Jesus to get Simon's attention because he was busy with business. And today it is hard for God to get the attention of men because men are busy with busy-ness. We are busy making money as bees are busy making honey. We are busy trying to get a university degree, busy trying to be famous, busy trying to boost our career, achieve our never-ending goals and be successful in our field, busy trying to be rich and happy, busy trying to make a frustrating relationship work, busy trying to make a name for ourselves.

Being too busy is costing us what matters most in our lives. Some of us are so busy with our business, career, and stuffs that we don't even have time for our loved ones. I used to think that those who are very busy to the level that they don't have time for anyone is just being selfish until I found some people who are too busy that they don't even have time to take care of themselves. Funny right?

We make our agenda, set goals, and draw plans for the day, the week, the month, the year, and God is not found in any of them. Our calendar is fully booked, our diary so occupied and there's no place for God in any of them. Even on Sundays that are considered to be worship day, we find it hard to give God two or three hours of service. Even while in a church service, our mind is so busy with stuff that at the end of the service we can't even remember what the pastor taught or what the preacher preached.

Jesus wants to reveal to us a lot about ourselves but we are missing it because we are very busy. We are too busy with a lot that what Romans 9:16 said never seems to cross our stubborn ears:

"So then it is not of him that willeth, nor of him that runneth, but of God that showeth mercy."

Your will to succeed can be very strong that you passionately run towards your vision and ideas without realizing that life is not fair, that it is not always the best that wins. The best contractor doesn't always get the million-dollar contracts. The best graduating student don't always get the best-paying jobs. The most intelligent student's don't always pass the exam. The best doctor doesn't always get to save all his patients from dying. The most beautiful ladies don't always get to marry the Mr. Right kind of husband. Having a strong will to succeed doesn't always guarantee success. Running hard towards your dream doesn't always mean you will get there. Having the best certificate doesn't always mean you will get the job you seek.

"I returned, and saw under the sun, that the race is not to the swift, nor the battle to the strong, neither yet bread to the wise, nor yet riches to men of understanding, nor yet favour to men of skill..." (Ecclesiastes9:11)

Until this happens, those who consider themselves to be the best don't ask themselves questions. It is when the swift loses the race when the wise (smart and intelligent) cannot see bread to eat when men of understanding and craft see they are financially bankrupt when men with great skills notice that the one who has lesser skill is selected over them that they begin to ask themselves the question, How did I fail at my best? What is happening?

CHAPTER 3:

FAILED AT YOUR BEST

There's always something in this life where you will consider yourself to be the best. Even if you don't assume that you are the best but you are very sure you are very good at something. It may be an innate gift, a learned skill, and ability you have acquired over time through training or something you studied and got certified to practice from a university.

You don't need to compete with anybody to decide if you are the best or not. If you do something that you love and it draws most of your time, energy, and passion, that's the best of you in expression. You don't need a title or world ranking list to be called the best in anything.

Your career can be your best; it can also be your job, business, ministry, or even a relationship you cherish so much. It captivates your heart and holds your attention; it draws your attention and focuses your energy. It is where your vision lies, what crowds your imagination and fills your dominant thought. It is a path you have taken towards where you want to be, a height you want to attain

Simons best was fishing. He could fish all day or all night without getting tired. From a young age, he was educated and certified in the art of fishing. He had a genetic advantage in fishing and he was very good at it that he even had a big ship for fishing. He lived in a time when there were no fish finders, GPS units, and other devices that aid fishing. There were no plastic float-ing worms, no sophisticated fishing boats, and motors yet he was successful in the fishing business because he was well acquainted with fishing craft.

From a very young age when he was not qualified to use nets yet, he was a good angler because he spent time mastering the skill of casting and looping. He knew how to get his knots to-gether for the braided super lines. He also knew fire line, spider wire, and Tuf-line. He was so good with the way he prepared his loop that he later founded a style other fishermen called Simon Loop and Simon Knot.

He understood the lifestyle and uniqueness of each fish; that all fishes need food, oxygen, and cover. Anyone who wants to be good at fishing must maximize on fishes need for food, oxygen, and cover. Simon understood how those three things work with respect to fishes. He knew when the wind is in his favor, the dir-ection of the wind is a determinant as well. Fishes follow micro-organisms carried downward by the push of the water and bigger fishes hunt the little fishes that feed on microorganisms.

Simon knew that fishes like bass move onto flats and lake edges to catch the sun early, so he always targeted the headwaters where there was impoundment. So if he was fishing for bass, he knew where to go that he would not find more bass or perch in a pound where bluegills are many. He understood that pickerel and pikes have sharp teeth, so when fishing for them, he must use a strong rod, hook, and leader that are resistant to bites and harder for fishes to detect than the main fishing line. He also under-stood how salmon, mackerel, trout, and other fishes behave indi-vidually. Most importantly, he understood the rule of fishing big fishes. He knew that when the big fish pulls, the fisherman doesn't but when the big fish doesn't pull, the fisherman pulls.

Simon didn't go to any school but he understood thermo-cline. He understood that temperatures of water change grad-ually, above and below the thermocline because there is always little oxygen below the thermocline which indicates that fishing below the thermocline is always poor so he targets his fishing above the thermocline where fishes stay to get oxygen.

WHAT HAVE YOU CAUGHT?

While I was still in high school, my school was about 10km from my house so daily I took public transport to my school to the point that I became friends with those commuter bus drivers that drove in that axis. These bus drivers and their conductors resumed work before 6 am and close around 8 pm or beyond on daily basis. They were definitely hard-working fellows.

Fifteen years after my high school graduation, I was coming back from the city where I was working and I still met those bus drivers and to my greatest surprise, they were not in any way better than the way they were fifteen years ago. In fact, many of them looked worse than they were fifteen years back. And that made me think, "What's wrong?" I know they work hard but there's no evidence of the hard work. I ask myself, "Is this what they are destined to do all the days of their lives?" These men have been fishing in the same river for fifteen years and it looks like they have caught nothing worthwhile enough?

Doing something for fifteen years at the same place and you have nothing to show for it should definitely make someone think. Maybe they never asked themselves this question.

After long years of hard work and toiling, after you have denied yourself a lot in life just to achieve a particular goal, after years of being busy with busy-ness, after you have cast your bread upon many waters as baits, after you have thrown nets upon many seas, sown different seeds into many presumed fertile grounds, you baited with huge capitals and leverages, you baited with your heart and body, you baited with what you cherish the most and what you consider your favorite, a day will come that you should halt at the junctions of reality check where you collapse to the chair and ask yourself this powerful soul searching question: What have I caught?

It is written that weeping may endure till night but joy comes in the morning. The night season of one's life is always long and painful, full of uncertainties, depression, and frustration. Your night time may be your studious and tedious time in the university when what kept you going is the hope of a morning that will come with a lucrative job after graduation. It may be your time as an apprentice and employee somewhere and you were hoping that your morning will come with independence, promotion, and its benefits.

Just at the edge of dusk you must wake up and ask yourself, How far and how well?

Even if you don't ask yourself that question, definitely situations will. People close to you will ask you. Your boss or even your colleagues will ask you. What do you have to show so far after all these years? Amid your activity, they will ask you where your productivity is. They will ask you directly or indirectly. Questions like:

At this age what have you achieved?

What is still holding you from getting married?

Ten years and you don't have a child yet, why?

Remember it is not an insult when people begin to ask you where your result is. It is because they have seen your night seasons and they are expecting your morning to come with joy and comfort.

But what will you do when your morning seems to have come but you see neither joy nor comfort?

A very similar scenario of what happened in Luke 5:1-5 happened in John 21:2-5 where Peter went fishing with some disciples and that night they caught nothing.

"But when the morning was come, Jesus stood on the shore: but the disciples knew not what it was Jesus. Then Jesus saith unto them, Children, have ye any meat? They answered him, No."

The same question is coming to you today:

Have you any meat (what satisfies your heart desires)?

Hi hustler, have you made your millions yet?

Hello beautiful lady, have you any husband yet?

Holla! Have you hit that big contract you are pursuing?

Hey. Graduate, have you gotten your dream job you're applying for?

Reflecting on this question can open your eyes to see that despite all your toil you still have not made a big catch yet. Or have you?

Maybe you used to make huge cash and catch before but right now nothing is in your net and it hurts when you look around you and sees people enjoying their catch but you have made none. You see them enjoying their meat, driving their new cars, having their weddings, playing with their children, living in the new houses they built, fulfilling their dreams, and basking in their accomplishments. And you look at your net to notice you have caught nothing and have no meat.

Have you ever been doing something in life and you are watching time at the same time because you feel you have a time limit? When you look at your empty net and look at your time and season it can be depressing. When a 40 years old beautiful single lady looks at herself that she has no husband and looks at her age, it has a way of destabilizing her emotions. When a man is 58 years, getting close to his retirement then he realizes that he has no house, no car, or worthy property he can call his own despite years of service it has a way of making him feel like a failure.

THE END OF THE ROPE

Truly, there is a stage in life, when you're not supposed to be seeking some things, when you are supposed to retire from the pursuit of your desires, sit back and enjoy the fruit of your labor. But if at this stage you look at your net and discover you have nothing and the time to achieve them has come and gone, the season to harvest has come and you have nothing to harvest, you have thrown your net all night but pulls up an empty net. It hurts.

It hurts more when you remember that you used to pull up your net previously and a lot would come out with it but at the moment nothing comes out at all or comes out very few especially when you know you have thrown it with your very best at the right place.

To fail at your worst is normal but to fail at your best is completely abnormal. When a champion wins, it is normal but when he loses, loses, again and again, something has gone wrong somewhere. It is painful to remember glory days. When you used to be the best at what you do when you were the expert at your art, the master of your craft, the champion in your field. But right now you are asking yourself, "What happened? Where am I getting it wrong? This used to work for me but why is it not working any longer."

You are using the same approach, same technique, applying the same principles, and yet you still not getting it. At this moment the best advice that comes to your head is to try a different approach and a different thing entirely. But does it help?

I believe Simon tried different approaches that night yet he couldn't catch a fish, he couldn't even catch a sick fish that wants to commit suicide so it was looking for an empty net where it would enter and kill itself, he changed his hook size, he changed his bait, he reset the net setting and changed position yet he made no catch. He rested and changed strategy severally yet he made no catch that's when he knew he had come to the end of the rope.

There is a time in our lives that to get what we want we do pull some strings, because normally pulling those strings always works, but sometimes you will pull the string and pull and pull till you come to the end of the rope. The end of the rope is when you have tried all you know and studied yet you can't get it right. The end of the rope is when you have done the best diagnosis, consulted the best doctors, and took every medication prescribed yet your health challenges fail to respond positively to treatment. The end of the rope is when a single lady has done all the sexy and romantic things she knows, tried applying the best fashion advice yet she can't attract, and keep a good relationship that will end in marriage. The end of the rope is when a couple has consulted the best marriage counselors, read the best books on relationship and marriage yet their relationship doesn't seem to be working. The end of the rope can be when you have gone through several therapy sessions and rehabilitation yet you are not getting better or coming out of that habit. The end of the rope is when you fail at your best despite your skills, gifts, charisma, academic qualification, and expertise which can't provide the solution to your problems.

Good news! The end of the rope is not the end of hope. At the end of the rope, people do two things. They either give up or they hang on.

BUT WHY GIVE UP?

I have never easily judged and condemn people who commit suicide without trying to understand what made them do it. I believe life is sweet that no matter how hard it may be, nothing can make one take his own life. But people who commit suicide don't wake up one day and decide to do it; they have been in a secret battle till they lost.

Their faith has been in a battle with their fears, their past, and present against their future, their guilt against their conviction, their despair against their hope, their frustration against their inspiration. The worst part is that they battle it alone secretly like a boxer in a Caged Ring match till they reach that point when they feel they have taken enough blows, their vision is battered that they can't see any other thing else except darkness, their creative hands hurt, their feet used for daring becomes exhausted. And hope, their only motivator who keeps telling them to fight one more round seems to have vanished like a round smoke puffed into the air, so they decide to throw in the towel. The light at the end of the tunnel is no longer there for them, the oasis has gone dry and the superman who saves the day is no longer coming so they decide the only way out is to take their own life.

Have you been there when you feel you are in a battle against something overwhelming, you against the world, your fear against your faith, your past against your present, and your present against your future? And then that moment when you think you are winning there comes a blow that throws you off your feet, you find yourself down again reeling in pain. And there is no one to throw in the lifeline to you. Everything around you is telling you to throw in the towel. And you find yourself at the end of the rope dangling like an old rag in between holding on or letting go to fall off. And there are a time when hanging on is exhausting because you no longer have the strength to hang on. If people dare tell you to hold on you get upset and the first question that comes to your bruised mouth is, Hold on to what again?

Sometimes we see people who give up as people of no or little faith. Many of them had faith but facts have fought their faith so hard that their faith is weakened. She believes that she will get pregnant one day but medical facts show her that she has reached menopause with other complications and there is no way she will take in at her age. The fact will show her couples who tried and failed, later settled for adoption.

He has a revelation that he will make it to destiny one day but his reality is quite depressing and here he is, watching his reality wrestle with his revelation. And statistics of people who have failed before him make him believe he doesn't stand a chance.

She has a strong moral status but statistics of failed relationship has hit her so bad that she has lowered her standard in order to get married. She has thrown away her virtues, values, and principles because of her previous relationship, and the ones before it failed because she held on to her values.

Statistics of failed relationships can make you stop believing in love, statistics of divorce cases in our present world can make you question the essence of marriage. It can make you give up on the good things you once believed about marriage. Ugly news on our media can make you give up on this beautiful world entirely. All these can push you to the edge that you scream, "I've had enough, and I'm packing my net to wash it. I am tired of fishing for what no longer exists and pursuing what I cannot get. I'm tire of everything. I'm tired of life."

But I wrote this book to tell you, don't wash your net yet, there is still hope, your help is still on the way and it is close to you. If you think you have nothing to hang on to, hang on to what God has for you that you have not seen yet.

A widow in Zarephath came to the end of her rope, she faced the fact that she had nothing to eat and no way to get food and her only hope was a handful of flour in a jar and a little oil in a jug which she would use to make a meal for her son to eat and die afterward. (1 King1 7:7-15).

And while she was about to wash her net, God sent her help in form of a prophet called Elijah and that encounter with a divine personality changed her story.

In Samuel 9, Saul and his servant were looking for his father Kish's lost ass but searching for the ass for many days and couldn't find it, Saul said, "Let's call it a day and go back."

The wise servant replied, "No, we can't give up now, we have come this far not to go back empty-handed. I know someone who can help us. Let's go meet a man of God."

And when they did meet the man of God, the young Saul discovered his destiny as the first king of Israel.

I know you are tired. Tired of life, tired of everything and everyone but why give up when help is on the way. Hang on there, till your help comes. Hope never fails. There is a great thing God has in store for you, you may not know exactly what it is but let it be your hope.

CHAPTER 4:
OFFERING THAT ENDS SUFFERING

"And he entered into one of the ships, which was Simons and PRAYED him that he would thrust out a little from the land. And he sat down and taught the people out of the ship." (Luke 5:3)

Most times when the help we want arrives, it doesn't always look exactly the way we expect it. A helping hand can come disguised as a demanding hand. Isn't it interesting that you can expect to receive from someone and the person is expecting from you too? The truth is this, when you expect to receive, you should also be ready to give as well.

I know it is better to sit down with our hands and legs crossed till our doorbell rings and we open the door to see the delivery man wearing Santa Claus red and white suit bearing our miracles in his hands with red ribbons wrapped around it. The truth is that Santa Claus doesn't always come to us; sometimes we pay a token to go and see him.

There was a little trick Santa Claus used to play on kids back in the days, he would give you candy and ask it back from you, and if you as a kid has a giving spirit that you extend your hand to give the candy back, he would give a nice toy.

THE MASTERS NEED

In life, exchange is as constant as change; you give what you have to get what you don't have. As long as the Law of Seedtime and Harvest do not cease, you must sow your seed if you must gather your harvest. Even God in his omnipotence observes the law of exchange that he gives to us as much as we are ready to give him no matter how little our gift may be. It is written, Give and it shall be given unto you...

It is very striking that Bible (KJV) stated that Jesus PRAYED to Simon to give him his boat. As much as it sounds as holy irony yet it beautifies the fact that God can demand something from us who besiege him day and night with our endless list of what we want for our selfish gratification. But how could the omnipotent God who created all things want something from us?

The earth is the Lords and the fullness thereof; the world and they that dwell therein, for he founded it upon the seas and established it upon the waters. Every beast of the forest is his and he owns the cattle upon a thousand hills. He cuts a channel for the torrents of rain, and a path for the thunderstorm, to water a land where no man lives, a desert with no one in it, to satisfy a desolate wasteland and make it sprout with grass. He satisfies the hunger of the young lions when they crouch in their dens or lie in wait in a thicket. He provides food for the raven when it's young cry out to Him and wander about for lack of food. He fed five thousand men with five loaves of bread and two fishes and had twelve baskets full of leftovers. And when he needed to pay his tax and his disciples tax he commanded a fish to bring it in its mouth because, *The silver is mine, and the gold is mine, saith the LORD of hosts.* **(Hag.2:8)**

So why does God demand something from us?

God doesn't demand anything from us because He needs it and can't get it anywhere else but He seems to be playing a similar game Santa Claus plays on kids. He has something bigger and better for us but first He wants to test our giving spirit. Whenever God wants to bless you, He would first test your giving spirit.

Blessing is free but to get blessed in a big way, you must first pass the test of Giving.

God cannot step down from his heavenly throne to come and enlarge His kingdom on earth when he has you and me. His main need is to enlarge His kingdom on earth, that all men will be saved and come to the knowledge of Him. And whosoever that can give in support of His course will provoke His miraculous hand.

So Jesus said to Simon, I need your ship, I want to use it to reach out to this multitude and teach them Gods word.

And Simeon gave Jesus his ship not knowing he has provoked his own breakthrough.

Today, Jesus is calling out to you who would give for the furtherance of His course on earth. Before you give up before you wash your net as Simon. I have a question for you. Can you give Jesus your ship?

I know you don't have Simons kind of ship to give yet you have something special to give: your time, your energy, your money, your property, your services are needed for the masters use. Can you give any of them?

It's what you have that you give and it's what you give that provokes Gods hand to give you in return. The blessing is in giving not in withholding. Never you think you are the sole sponsor of Gods kingdom when you give, you are too small for that, you are giving to unlock the blessings Gods kingdom has for you.

ACTIVATE YOUR ANSWERS

And Elijah said unto her, Fear not, go and do as thou hast said: but make me, therefore, a little cake first, and bring it unto me, and after make for thee and for thy son. For thus saith the LORD God of Israel, The barrel of meal shall not waste, neither shall the cruse of oil fail, until the day that the LORD sendeth rain upon the earth. And she went and did according to the saying of Elijah; and he, and her house, did eat many days. And the barrel of meal wasted not, neither did the cruse of oil fail, according to the Word of the Lord which he spake by Elijah.

(1King 17:13-16)

Whenever I read this, I scream, "Oh my God, what a faith!" I don't know how many people can do such a thing in our present-day world. Our present-day folks who elevate reasoning over faith don't consider it logical to give the last thing they have or close their bank account for God just to receive a miracle.

Seriously it doesn't make sense to give your last meal to a man because he is called a man of God. Anyway, things of God don't make sense. No physical senses can comprehend the tenses God uses to perform miracles. Tell someone to give to a servant of God these days. The first thing they will say, Thieves, they have come again. What they only care about is their own belly.

Your solution is in the hand of someone and that person is called a man or a woman of God, he or she may not necessarily have an ecclesiastical title, she may not be a graduate of a notable theology school, he may not dress in a cassock with a white collar around his neck, and a long miter on his head. Fortunately, God can use anyone and can send anyone to be a blessing to you.

We have a generation that attacks men of God because they don't understand that God attaches his blessings to those men and women who stand in His office, so they ignorantly blast who is supposed to bless them. I understand the fact that many have suffered under the hand of fake preachers who tagged themselves as men of God. They have lost a fortune because they thought they are giving it to God. I understand there are a lot of leopards disguised as shepherds, criminal suspects who pose as prophets, pastors who are just actors out to entertain the world with their sugar-coated words just to be popular yet there are still real men of God out there with true anointing upon their lives. Jesus said by their fruit you will know them, if all you are seeing is their gift you will make mistakes because gifts can be faked but fruits cant. If you are not seeing the fruit yet, give it time it will reveal itself.

The problem is not the fake prophets; the problem is that you are not perceptive enough to differentiate the true from the false.

You need to be like the Samaritan woman who on her encounter with Jesus was perceptive enough to recognize who she was speaking with.

"The woman saith unto him, Sir, I perceive that thou art a prophet." **(John4:19)**

This perceptive spirit is what we are lacking in our days. That's why a lot of people are being deceived. A lot of sheep are being devoured by the wolves because they don't know the voice of the shepherd. Some of us allow our desperation for miracles to override our perceptive spirit. And since desperate people do desperate things they can easily fall into traps.

"And it fell on a day, that Elisha passed to Shunam, where was a great woman, and she constrained him to eat bread. And so it was, that as oft as he passed by, he turned in thither to eat bread. And she said unto her husband, Behold now, I perceived that this is a holy man of God, which passed by us continually. Let us make a little chamber, I pray thee on the wall; and let us set for him there a bed, and a table, and a stool, and a candlestick; and it shall be, when he cometh to us, that he shall turn in thither." **(2Kings4:8-10)**

This great woman here was not sure who Elisha was but she gave herself time to sense spiritually who Elisha was. This woman needed a child and she had given up on having one. She must have washed her net since her womb was not catching anything. But when she perceived that Elisha was a man of God she gave an offering that activated her miracles.

Giving is not what you should do because preachers pep talked you into it, it is not something you should do with the mentality of a money-doubler or with the idea of a gambler. Giving is what you should do under two conditions

First, you give because God commanded you to give. It was God who commanded the widow of Zarephath to sustain Elijah (1 King17:9). So she responded to Gods command. If a preacher walks up to you and says, God said you should give me this or that.

The question you should ask yourself is: Has God said anything to me concerning this? Do I have a confirmation of what he said in my spirit?

Nobody has the monopoly of hearing from God. So let the God who spoke to him confirm to you before you give. God is your God and his God too. God didn't only speak to Elijah He spoke to the woman too in her spirit. Now God can command you to give your substance to His servant or His church.

Secondly, you give in faith to fill a righteous need. You may not hear any voice that commands you to give but you can give in faith to meet up a godly need. You give to support a kingdom project, to support missionary work, give to the needy, and for charity. Abraham was a man who knows how to give to fill a righteous need.

"And Abraham ran unto the herd, and fetched a calf tender and good, and gave it unto a young man; and he hasted to dress it. And he took butter, and milk, and the calf which he had dressed, and set it before them; and he stood by them under the tree, and they did eat. And they said unto him, where is Sarah thy wife? And he said, Behold, in the tent. And he said, I will certainly return unto thee according to the time of life; and lo, Sarah thy wife shall have a son. And Sarah heard it in the tent door, which was behind him." **(Genesis 18:7-10)**

Abraham is a model when it comes to giving in faith, he had trained his spiritual senses to perceive spiritual personality and he never missed to maximize such opportunities. That's why when he met Melchizedek in Genesis 14:20, he sensed that the man was a divine personality and he paid tithe to him which brought eternal blessings to him and his descendants. He paid tithe when there's no law on paying tithe and no one commanded him to pay tithe but he perceived in his spirit that tithing is a spiritual exercise and an act of gratitude.

So when Abraham met these strangers he knew by divine wisdom that they were not mere strangers but divine personalities on an earthly mission. And this is where we miss it, we mix up the personality of a man with his office, the office of a man is different from his personality, you may not like a man or respect him as a person but the office he represents has the power and authority to give you the answers you seek. Look at what Jesus said about giving to a man of God not because of his personality as a man but because of his divine office:

"He that receiveth a prophet in the name of a prophet shall receive a prophet's reward; and he that receiveth a righteous man in the name of a righteous man shall receive a righteous man's reward." **(Matthew 10:41)**

You may not like the governor of your state as a person but his signature can solve your biggest problem. You can criticize the president of your nation and disagree with him politically as much as you like yet his recommendation can sit you in a position that will change your story. You may not like a prophet as a person but your prosperity is tired to his prophet office as 2Chronicles 20:20 stated: *Believe in the LORD your God, so shall ye be established; believe his prophets, so shall ye prosper.*

One way to invoke the benevolence of a man in a great office is through gifts. Two men enter the office of a commissioner seeking a government contract and each of them is qualified for the contract. One comes pleading to get the contract because he has bills to pay and debts to clear. Another comes with a gift of a bottle of champagne to make merry the heart of the commissioner. Who do you think will get the contract? When you come to receive, don't come with your hand empty. Truly, your gift makes way for you.

"A man's gift maketh room for him, and bringeth him before great men." **(Proverbs 18:16)**

Abraham had heard the promise of a son repeated times without number in his wrinkled ears, he had several divine encounters, made sacrifices upon many alters yet the manifestation he anticipated was far-fetched until he offered that calf as a delicious meal out of faith to those men he perceived to be divine personality his answer was activated. That gift of faith provoked God to fast forward the fulfillment of his promise to him. He brought his thirty years of waiting to an end.

You got to understand that promises are free but breakthroughs come with a cost. So right now you have to cook for God your delicacies. Unfortunately, He doesn't eat meat, butter, cheese, and milk. He eats praises and worship.

THE MAN WITH THE SOLUTION

In the book of 2 Kings 3:8, there is a scenario of three kings who were out for war; everything was going out well as planned until the unexpected happened. Nobody likes the unexpected because it is always uncomfortable handling what you didn't plan for. The unexpected is always the show stopper, the joy killer, the party crasher, and the nemesis of every goal-getter and it always shows up uninvited.

These kings had to entertain this visitor in the middle of nowhere. They had to switch to plan B, C, and D yet their options dried up like an oasis in the Sahara Desert. This visitor would determine the success of their campaign because their soldiers, camels, and horses needed water to survive. It can make loyal soldiers rebel against their commander, it can make horses refuse to go the direction their rider is pointing, it can make the most decorated of warriors weary.

The visitor was Drought.

"And the king of Israel said, Alas! That the LORD hath called these three kings together, to deliver them into the hand of Moab!" **(2 Kings 3:10).**

Those were the words of King Jehoram when he found himself at the end of the rope. And confessing negatively is the last thing you should do when you find yourself in a hopeless situation.

It was only King Jehoshaphat who realized that they had come to the end of their rope and hanging up would be as dangerous as letting go because the rope would soon snap, so he resolved to find an immediate solution.

King Jehoshaphat understood that most times when you need answers, you don't look anyway, there's a right place to look. He understood that answer is with God no matter how hopeless it may look. It is only over when God says it is over. So King Jehoshaphat asked in verse 11:

"Is there not here a prophet of the Lord that we may inquire of the LORD by him? And one of the kings of Israel's servants answered and said, Here is Elisha the son of Shaphat, which poured water on the hands of Elijah. And Jehoshaphat said, The Word of the Lord is with him..."

The word of the LORD marks the true prophet, not the title, not the visions, not the signs and omen but the Word. There are a lot of prophets and seers who can see your problems but they cannot proffer a solution. They can ring the bell, dance in circles on one leg, toss their head back and forth like Lucky Dube, call your full name while you are still at the door, tell you the day you were born, the color of your underwear, who wants to kill you and who is the cause of your problem but they can't give you the word of the LORD.

We have counselors, life coaches, therapists who can put you through sessions of counseling and therapy, they give you 5 ways to do this, 7 methods to achieve that, 10 steps to come out of stuff, 12 keys to unlock the unknown doors, 30 principles to apply, 50 laws to obey yet the word of the LORD is not with them. Sorry to tell you there are situations when counseling and therapy sessions cannot help you, the only thing that can help you is the Word of the Lord because the Word is the solution and answer you need.

King Jehoshaphat understood what they needed was the prophet with the word of the Lord, so he was not looking for the most famous prophet, nor the preacher with the highest number of the congregation, the general overseer with ultra-modern cathedral church, the minister with the highest number of social media followers. He was looking for Thus says the LORD....Because if the Lord says, everything must fall in place. That's why when Elisha was mentioned, he said, *The Word of the LORD is with him...*because the Word is the answer.

OFFERING OF WORSHIP

And when the three kings stood before the man of God, right there I understand what it means to be a true man of God and another way to recognize a true man of God. The presence of Jehoram King of Israel provoked Elisha that he lost his spiritual alignment with heaven. Elisha had the option to speak as man and his visitors would believe him, but a true man of God speaks not what he feels, nor does he speak neither by the state of his emotions nor by the statistics of what he knows that works or won't work but only what God commands him to say. And to do that, he had to tune his spirit to hear from God and connect to the heavenly frequency.

He asked them to bring a minstrel (musician) to him because when a minstrel plays a song of praise and worship, it would create a God-filled atmosphere which is the best atmosphere to hear from God. As a child of God, it is your right to hear from God because He is your Father. And you can create the atmosphere to hear from him right there at your home or at your office or even inside your car. You enter Gods gate with the key of thanksgiving and his court with the key of praise **(Psalm 100:4).**

We always want the Spirit of God to minister to us but we don't know how to minister to the LORD. If we want God to speak we must learn to minister to him.

"As they ministered to the Lord, and fasted, the Holy Ghost said..." **(Acts 13:2)**

And when the minstrel played (ministered), the Spirit of God who is the Spirit of the solution came upon Elisha and he prophesied the Word of the Lord concerning the solution. And what was the solution? Elisha asked them to make an offering.

"And it came to pass in the morning, when the meat offering was offered, that behold, there came water by the way of Edom, and the country was filled with water." **(2Kings 3:20)**

There is an offering that can end your suffering. When what you have is not enough to be your harvest make it a seed and sow it. Your five loaves of bread may be small, offer it to God and watch your gift feed five thousand. When you come to the end of the rope make sure you have an offering ready, you will see how it will open the door of abundance and miracles to you.

On Tuesday evening in May 2020, I witnessed something I have never seen in my years as a medical sales representative. I visited a customer around 6:10 pm, I noticed the pharmacy was operational but was locked from inside and I was told I could not enter until 7 pm. So all customers and visitors had to wait or go and come back later. I enquired what was going on and one of the staff a pharmacist told me they were having a fellowship inside the pharmacy. I had two other colleagues of mine who were very angry at the idea of using business premises for religious purposes which should keep them waiting till the fellowship was over, so they left and waited in a nearby bar. I told the pharmacist I would join the fellowship so he let me in and I participated in the prayers and communion led by the owner of the pharmacy shop.

Out of curiosity, I asked the pharmacist what inspired this unusual event. He told me it is not unusual, it is what they do every Tuesday of the week; they suspend all business activity and use it for God. He told me a story of how their pharmacy was robbed and virtually every drug in the pharmacy was stolen that they have to start the business again from the scratch. And the owner of the pharmacy made a vow to God to be offering his pharmacy shop as a venue for worship. By doing that they were able to recover, bounce back in business and grow to the height they have reached.

The director of the pharmacy had an option to watch his net and go back to his village, he had the right to say, "You know what, this business is not for me. I quit." But he realized that he has been very busy with business that he ignored God, and like Simon who offered his ship to the ministry of Jesus Christ, this young man offered his pharmacy store to the work of God.

What will you offer to God to provoke the miracle or breakthrough you seek. Don't say I have nothing to give. Every giver knows he or she has something to give. It may be your talent, your gift, your services, your property, etc. Even if you don't know what to do, there's something the Lord is demanding from you, listen and you will hear time saying, Give me this area of your life.

There was a time in my life my offering to God was to serve as the pastor's driver. Every Sunday morning, I drove my car to pick the pastor for service and after church service; I did drive my pastor back to his house since he had no car at that time. It was my offering to the work of God. And I know the breakthroughs that act of service brought to my life.

After you have given to God, listen and hear him give you His word that will bring the solution to your problems.

CHAPTER 5.

AT THY WORD

*"Now when he had left speaking, he said unto Simon, Launch
out into the deep, and let down your nets for a draught.
And Simon answering said unto him, Master, we have
toiled all the night, and have taken nothing: nevertheless,
at thy word I will let down the net." (Luke 5:4-5)*

Most times people don't get the miracle they need from God, not because they ask amiss, not because they are dogs seeking to eat children's bread, but they have a wrong attitude towards receiving. People tend to get it wrong when it comes to receiving despite they have prayed right. They come into God's presence with out-stretched hands instead of with open ears. They expect God to open his hand meanwhile God has opened his mouth to speak.

They stand before a man of God and expect him to lay his hand or his leg on them instead of listening to hear what God is saying through him. They are more satisfied with a holy commotion than a simple word of solution. So they feel God is at work more when the anointed one cries out in prayer, screams, shrieks, quake, and fumes like an exhausted old generator than when he says gently, "Go and do this according to the word of the Lord."

No wonder Naaman came before Elisha with gifts of gold and silver, what the book of Ecclesiastes called a sacrifice of fools and he got so disappointed when the man of God asked him to go to Jordan and wash.

"Keep thy foot when thou goest to the house of God and be more ready to hear, than to GIVE sacrifice of fools: for they consider not that they do evils." **(Ecclesiastes 5:1)**

After you have fasted and prayed, after you have sowed big seeds and met the needs of thousands with huge sacrifices, after you have done your charity and philanthropic work, after you must have exercised faith. One thing you must do is to LISTEN.

If you must receive from God, you must have open ears.

The answer you are expecting from God may not be delivered to you like a package you ordered from Amazon or Jumia. Nor can it happen like magic conjured by the wand of a powerful wizard of the first order. No. It cant come to you like a wish you made to Genie after you have rubbed the golden lamp. It will come to you like a word of solution.

The solution you are expecting from God can come as:

- Instruction.
- Direction

Most people Jesus healed in the Bible; He didn't lay his hands on them nor pray for them. He gave them his word of solution.

To most people, he said, *According to your faith be it unto you.*

To the leper in **Matthew 8:4**, he said, *Go thy way, show thyself to the priest and offer the gift that Moses commanded, for a testimony unto them.*

To the paralytic, he said, *Arise, take up thy bed and go unto thine house.***(Matthew 9:6).**

To the man born blind, he said, *Go wash (your face) in the pool of Siloam.***(John9:7)**

To those without wine at the wedding in Cana Galilee, he said, *Fill the jars with water... Now draw some out and take it to the master of the banquet.***(John 2:7-8)**

To the frustrated and hopeless man by the pool of Bethsaida, he said, *Rise, take up thy bed and walk.***(John5:8)**

To Peter, who saw himself as a failed disciple and went back to fishing yet failed again in fishing, He said, *Cast the net on the right side of the ship, and yea shall find.***(John 21:6)**

So before you give up remember that the master has a word for you and until you get it never say never. He has the final say, he is the great umpire and the game is not over until he blows the final whistle. The game is still on for you, you can score your winning shot, all you need is to listen to hear when, how, and where to shoot it. For years you have been talking to yourself and listening to people talk to you, just look where it got you. Now, you should let God speak to you and you need to listen if you really want to see results.

DIG YOUR DITCHES

If the instructions come and you must be ready to carry them out and here is an instruction you must carry out.

Back to the stories of the three kings in 2Kinga 3, before they got the miracle that saved the day for them, the man of God Elisha gave them a word of instruction.

And he said, "Thus saith the LORD, Make this valley full of ditches." And that is a powerful word of the instruction right there.

If you need your miracle, you must be ready to dig your own ditch. You need to create a gap. You need to create a space to receive. Miracle does not drop on a place that already fills up. You need to prepare a place for your miracle. Your heart and your hand must be open to receive. If unforgiveness, pride, guilt, and bitterness are occupying a big place in your heart you need to empty yourself of those toxins to receive. You must let go in order to let in.

Giving is a way of creating space in your hand to receive. If you withhold, your hand will be so filled that it cannot receive.

Give to create a space to receive.

If you need new clothes empty your wardrobe of old clothes that occupy spaces where new clothes will stay.

Don't expect a new car when you have not created a space for it. If you want a car, get a garage. Build one if you don't have, or rent an apartment that has a garage. Make sure you have a parking space for your new car; you can't carry it on your head. Just create space for your blessing that is coming.

A bird that is expecting new chicks first builds an empty nest before the eggs come. If you need a baby, you need to create space for a baby in your life, the baby has not come but you can buy baby kinds of stuff, get your entire house ready for a baby because you have faith the baby will soon come.

If you need a husband, create a space for a man in your life by forgiving men and all they did to you. When you sleep, sleep at the edge of the bed leaving space for where he will be sleeping beside you, while you visualize him holding you all through the night as your husband. Leave space for where he will hang his clothes, have a seat for him at the dining table, cook with a husband in mind. Don't let your ex occupy the space where your new husband will live.

If you need more congregations in your ministry or more attendance in your school, get a bigger apartment to buy more chairs because you are creating a space for thousands who are on their way.

Just dig your ditches, don't worry how it will be filled because God is the filler. Sometimes you don't need to dig a ditch in your life because there's already an existing ditch, space, and emptiness in your life. And all this time while you have been trying to fill it with something that can never fill it. Emotional emptiness. Financial emptiness. Social emptiness in form of loneliness. Spiritual emptiness. You are hungry but you dont know what you are hungry about. Thirsty but can't pinpoint what makes you feel so dry. Craving for things you can't define. And you have been trying different kinds of stuff to quench it and fill the emptiness in you but none of those things can fill the emptiness but God.

Not alcohol. Not sex. Not narcotics. Not partying and beaching. Not even money can fill the empty place in your life but God.

"For thus saith the LORD, Ye shall not see wind, neither shall ye see rain; yet that valley shall be filled with water, that ye may drink, both ye, and your cattle, and your beast...And it came to pass in the morning, when the meat offering was offered, that behold, there came water by the way of Edom, and the country was filled with water." **(2Kings 3:17,20)**

Create a space, dig your ditch, don't worry about how it will be filled, God owes you no explanation, no scientific proof, and no philosophical deduction on how it will be done; your only business is to follow the instruction. God is the filler. God will fill it because He is the God that fills the emptiness.

When Moses first built the tabernacle in Exodus 40:34, 35 the LORD filled the tabernacle with a cloud of glory. When Solomon built the magnificent temple, the glory of the LORD filled it that the priests could not stand to minister **(1 Kings 8:11)**

In Acts of the Apostles 2, the helpless, lonely, and terrified disciples were in the upper room in one accord until God came and filled the house they were with a sound from heaven as of rushing mighty wind and they were all filled with Holy Ghost.

"But as truly as I live, all the earth shall be filled with the glory of the LORD." **(Numbers 14:21)**.

Our God is the filler, so do you have something he will fill for you? Do you have a space he will fill, an empty ditch you dug that he will fill? Are you hungry enough to be filled by Him?

If you want God to fill you with something great, become an empty vessel for those who hunger and thirst after righteousness shall be filled. **(Matthew 5:6)**

If you don't have enough space I mean enough vision, enough

goals, enough ideas, enough creativity, go and borrow some more because God can fill them all.

"Then he said, Go, borrow thee vessels abroad of all thy neighbors, even empty vessels; borrow not a few." **(2Kings 4:3).**

The size of your net, vessel, and barrel matters because it decides how much you will get in return. The number of your empty vessels is the number he will fill with oil. The number of your barrels filled with water is the number he will turn to wine. The bigger your net the bigger he will fill it with fishes. The bigger your frying pan, the bigger the fishes you will get to fry.

Don't have few visions, scanty goals, short foresight, and meager ideas. The greater they are the greater God can fill them. The bigger your hands are; the better God can fill them. The larger your heart the more God can fill it with wisdom. The bigger your mind the bigger he will fill it with powerful ideas.

He is always the God of In between places. He was in between the two thieves on the cross of Calvary; He is in between the cherubim of the Ark of the Covenant. He is the bridge for you to cross from hell to heaven, from sin to righteousness, from pain to paradise, from where you are coming from to where you are going to. In between your past and your future, let God fill it. In between who you were and who you want to be, let God fill it because he is the gap-filling God.

He is the one that will fill your house with good things (Job.22:18).

He fills your mouth with laughter and your lips with rejoicing (Job.22:21).

"And they did eat, and were all filled." **(Luke9:17)**

CAN YOU GO DEEPER?

Another powerful way God brings his solution is through a

word of direction. What you are looking for is not everywhere, there is a particular place where your solution lies, and all you need is a direction to that place. Your miracle, breakthrough, and blessings are not everywhere it is in an exact position. So positioning is a powerful key in discovering your destiny and miracle.

Jesus said to Simon, *"Launch out into the deep, and let down your nets for a drought."* **(Luke5:4)**

Sometimes many of us think we have a life well figured out until life starts getting uncomfortable and confusing because what was meant to be a temporal position for us, we accepted it as a permanent destination. You may be like a whale who grew up in an aquarium; growing up in it was comfortable, living and working there has always been favorable until you outgrow the aquarium and you never know you did, then what used to be fun start becoming frustrating, what you once found accommodating becomes suffocating that you notice you can no longer tolerate what you used to celebrate. Then you begin to lose interest in things that used to be of great interest to you. Gradually it becomes clear to you that you are not getting enough time again, enough space, enough privacy, enough love, enough of your dreams, enough of all your heart desires again and it becomes clear to you that you are frustrating yourself with shallow waters meanwhile you are destined for deeper waters.

And the best thing to do is to quit the aquarium and delve into a deep ocean. You are destined for deep waters it is high time you should stop frustrating yourself with shallow waters. You cannot maximize who you are in a place that minimizes you. The shallow place can be a comfortable place, it puts food on your table, it pays your bill, it gives you a form of security and makes you feel relevant but I hate to break it to you the time has come for you quit it. It used to work for you but right now it is no longer working, accept the reality and quit the shallow place.

You know the relationship is shallow but you are hoping it will get better and deeper one day and it is now close to a decade yet everything appears the same. You keep having relationships with shallow men who will make love to you but won't love you, they date you but won't make you their life mate then when you finally get hurt, you end up blaming all men. Staying because you are expecting things to change means you want to suffocate yourself.

As a fisherman, you may have spent your lifetime fishing on the shallow water but it is time for you to go deeper. It may be the same river you have been fishing in for years but what you are looking for you cannot get it again on the surface, the fishes have left the shallow places and they are now in the deeper place. Gold and precious minerals of the earth are not found on the surface of the stratosphere. They lie deep in the heart of the earth. If you need them, you need to dig deeper.

Going deeper doesn't necessarily mean changing location and vocation, it doesn't mean changing places and people, it can also mean staying in the same field you have been working on for years. The same city. The same business. The same career. The same ministry. The same company. The same relationship. No need to change anything or anyone. Just quit the superficial and launch into the deep.

Before you quit, stop and ask yourself: how deep am I in this? Am I deep enough or should I launch further deeper?

Listen!

The deep is calling and you can feel it though you may not understand it. Deeper knowledge. Deeper experience. Deeper training. Deeper love. Deeper insight and foresight. They are drawing you like a latent magnet. Something is calling you to quit being local and go global because your destiny transcends the national level, it extends to the international level. If you don't respond to the deep, the shallow place will frustrate you. You started failing at your best because you have outgrown the shallow place.

The frustration can make you miserable as you start throwing an unnecessary tantrum, antagonizing everyone around you, blaming everyone for everything, withdrawing from people who care for you, hurting people who love you because to you their love is choking you. They are not your problem; your problem is that you are frustrating yourself in what or where you have out-grown.

There's something you should know that you haven't known. There is a deeper experience you should seek that you have not sought maybe because you have so much affinity for the familiar to the extent that contempt is sitting between you and your miracle. When you think you know something or some-one too much, such over-familiarity can make you miss the best of them. You can lose your lover because you are overly famil-iar with him or her that you no longer see the reward you will get when you go deeper with them. You are busy doing the same thing for years that you fail to realize that it has become boring and clumsy. You are like Samson you trust so much in one method that always works for you that you fail to realize that one day it may disappoint you as you shake yourself to get results but your hair is gone.

Like Samson said, *"I will go out as other times before, and shake myself."* **(Judges 16:21).**

Well, you can go out and shake yourself but once the grace to get the result at that level finishes, you hit a rock bottom. We have a way of being confident and trusting in what always works for us that we dent know when we deplete the grace of operating at that level. We get complacent at the level where we get results to the extent that when things stop working we get stuck. Don't get stuck in the state of a plateau.

It is over in the level of shallowness but not over in the deeper level. Why not go deeper?

NEVERETHELESS

"And Simeon answering said unto him, Master, we have toiled all the night, and have taken nothing: nevertheless at thy word I will let down

the net." **(Luke 5:5)**

You may have reached that level of a plateau where you don't see anything farther or deeper. Like Simon you have every reason to object to the directions or instructions given to you because to you, you have tried it all before and it didn't work.

It doesn't matter what happened before, what you did, and what you didn't do. It doesn't matter where you have been, who has been there with you, who helped you, and who didn't help you. It doesn't matter the professionals you have consulted. The best place where you sought help. The methods you applied. It doesn't matter how long your night has lasted. It doesn't matter how many times you have failed and the places you have failed. It doesn't matter who hurt you and who left you when you needed them most. All of them don't matter again. You must learn how to put nevertheless to all of them.

What matters now is that the Master has spoken and everything will align to the word of the Master. Light came from nowhere and pushed away darkness because He spoke. The storm stopped because He hushed it. Leprosy disappeared because He commanded it to go. Demons fled at the sight of Him. The dead came back to life because the grave heard His voice and released the ones it was holding. So when the Master speaks suspend your excuses, and say this powerful word as Simon said, "Nevertheless."

Nevertheless, your pain that brought no gain. Nevertheless, your labors were not favored. Nevertheless, the cost of your lost investments. Nevertheless, your failed relationships and your betrayed friendships. Nevertheless, the application you have submitted in a thousand places and none has contacted you. Nevertheless, the things that stopped working for you. Nevertheless, the doctor said the sickness is incurable. Nevertheless, the medications you have taken over time prescribed by renowned physicians and powerful people who have prayed for you. Nevertheless, the fact staring at your face like the ugly face of your hater. Nevertheless, what the statistics say.

His word is the greatest authority in the universe so everything responds to it. The earth was created by the word and the earth and all that is in it respond to the word. The elements of creations respond to the words. The heavenly bodies respond to the word. When He speaks everything responds to his voice.

"The voice of the LORD is upon the waters: The God of glory thundereth: the LORD is upon many waters. The voice of the LORD is powerful; the voice of the LORD is full of majesty. The voice of the LORD breaketh the cedars; yea, the LORD breaketh the cedars of Lebanon. He maketh them also to skip like a calf; Lebanon and Sirion like a young unicorn. The voice of the LORD divideth the flames of fire. The voice of the LORD shaketh the wilderness; the LORD shaketh the wilderness of Kadesh. The voice of the LORD maketh the hinds to calve, and discovereth the forest: and in his temple doth every one speak of his glory." **(Psalm 29:9)**

During creation, darkness heard his voice and gave way to light. Chaos heard his voice and gave way for nature. Nature heard his voice and the water was separated from dry ground. The water heard his voice and brought forth aquatic living creatures. The earth heard his voice and brought forth vegetation. The red sea heard his voice and divided. The fish that swallowed Jonah heard his voice and vomited who it was holding. Fishes came to the net of Simon because they heard His voice. Why won't your situation respond when they hear His voice?

Contracts will hear His voice and come to you. The right man will hear His voice and come to marry you. Your barren womb will hear His voice and open to conceiving. Cancer will hear His voice and cancel itself out of your life. Depression will hear His voice and regress from your life. Wealth will hear His voice of prophecies and come to fill you with possessions and properties.

BEAUTIFUL SHOE

A young lady who was a faithful Christian cried to her pastor one day. She complained that she had been faithful in God's work over the years but why hasn't God rewarded her with a husband and she was getting older in her early 40s.

Her pastor looked at her and was moved with compassion; he held her and prayed for her. While he was praying for her, God gave him a word of solution to her.

He asked her, "Do you have a new stiletto you bought recently?"

"Yes sir." She replied bewildered.

"Wear that stiletto and a beautiful gown that will match it. Drive to this hotel (the name withheld) by 7:30 pm and sit by the reception."

"But sir, if I go there what will I be doing?" She asked still confused.

The pastor got a little bit annoyed. "Just do as the Lord directs."

The lady left, when she reached home she tried to figure out what her pastor told her but she couldn't. Nevertheless, she decided to do as she was told.

He dressed up in her best gown, put on her new stiletto like Cinderella and she drove down to the hotel.

She sat down at the reception with a bottle of water in her hand, and she couldn't find a connection between what she told her pastor and what she was asked to do. She waited till 7:30 pm and nothing happened. She picked her phone and called her pastor and said to him it is now 7:30 pm and nothing has happened. Her pastor asked her to wait a little longer.

She waited another 1 hour; she picked her phone and called her pastor again.

"Sir, you said I should wait here and I've waited over an hour and nothing has happened. I even look stupid sitting here. Should I go back?"

"What did I tell you to do? Do according to the instruction." The pastor replied.

"But sir…"

"Young woman, don't leave there and come back to me without a testimony." The pastor interrupted and hung up on her.

The lady had to obey the instruction from God through her pastor. Around 9 pm. A foreign sailor that lodged in the hotel wanted to check out. He came down to the reception and saw her sitting on a sofa by the reception; he looked at her and said:

"Beautiful shoes."

He went out and came to the reception because he forgot something, he looked at her again and said:

"Beautiful shoes."

She didn't reply to any of his comments but just smiled.

The foreign sailor came back and repeated beautiful shoes the third time. She smiled back and said, "Thank you, sir."

"May I know the beautiful lady wearing these beautiful shoes?" The handsome sailor added.

He asked for her number and she gave him. He asked her out on a date. The rest is a love story that ended in a beautiful marriage.

There's nothing the word of the LORD cannot do in your life. Stop trying to understand how. Stop asking for the explanation and details of everything. Take God by His word. When God speaks, don't add 'But' to it. Take Him by His word and you will get an oversized miracle.

CHAPTER 6
SOMETHING BEYOND YOU

"And when they had this done, they inclosed a great multitude of fishes: and their net brake. And they beckoned unto their partners, where were in the other ship, that they should come and help them. And they came, and filled both the ships, so that they began to sink." (Luke 5:6-7)

From the text above you will notice there is a change in the pronouns used. It changed from 'he' to 'they'. The attention moved from Simon to his team of fishermen. What God is about to do in your life is beyond you. His blessings are beyond you and your household.

Life is not all about you. The sun does not shine on you alone neither does the rain falls for you and your family alone. God is not satisfied with your life of selfishness where the only thing you care about is – me, myself, and I.

When people pray to be blessed, it is more of their selfish interest, for personal gratification and aggrandizement. God wants to fill your cup because He is the Filler but he wants a cup that will overflow. He is not in the business of feeling the cup half-way then sit back and listen to the argument of whether it is half filled or half empty. He wants to fill a cup that will overflow. He wants to feed the five thousand till they are filled and there would be leftovers. He doesn't mind if his children will drop some bread crumbs for dogs to feed on under the table. God is not a waster. He is an overflowing God.

OVERSIZE MIRACLE

"The LORD shall open unto thee his good treasure, the heaven to give the rain unto thy land in his season, and to bless all the work of thine hand: and thou shalt lend unto many nations, and thou shalt not borrow." **(Deuteronomy 28:12)**

In the previous chapter, we discussed the need for you to enlarge your capacity. If you are digging ditches you should dig so much deep ditches because He will fill them all. If you are to borrow a vessel, borrow so many vessels because He will fill them all. If you are to fill the water pots, fill enough water pots to the brim because He is going to turn them all to wine. He has enough fishes to fill your ship and any ship you will add to your ship. His plan for you isn't only to give you as far as you see and as fat as you can hold, He wants to give you an oversize miracle that only you cannot carry.

Simon prayed for a miracle but his net and ship were too small to carry the miracles God released to him. God wants to release a miracle of blessings that is so big that it will break your net. He wants to release to you a record-breaking breakthrough. It is something far beyond what you've ever seen before. Eyes have not seen, ears have not heard, and no heart has ever conceived the kind of blessings He wants to give you. But if your net is small and weak it will break.

If you don't have the capacity to hold what God is about to release to you, it will break you. There is a job or contract God wants to give you and if you don't have the right mental capacity it will break you down. There is a business breakthrough God can release to you and if you don't have the ethical capacity it can crash your capital. The truth is that you can't handle oversize blessings and miracles alone. You need to build a relationship capacity in order to be able to hold it.

Simon had to invite other partners and add ships to his ship to carry his oversize blessings. You need to grow to the level of having a team to handle what God wants to give you because it is too big that you can't handle it alone. You need to join other ships to your ship and that is called Partnership.

A cup can go alone when it is empty or half full. But when a cup is filled to the brim it needs the service of a saucer. God doesn't only want to fill your cup he wants to fill your cup to overflow till the saucer benefits. It is the destiny of the cup to carry the water or the wine and it is the destiny of the saucer to carry the cup. You may be the cup and someone else is destined to be your saucer. God is not only interested in blessing you. He wants to bless your destiny helpers too. He wants to bless people around you. He wants your employees and employers who help you carry your visions to benefit from His blessings in your life.

The blessings on Abraham overflowed to Lot his cousin. The house of Potiphar benefited from the blessing of God on Joseph. Naaman was blessed with healing because of the Jewish housemaid in his house who carried the blessings of Abraham. You are a bundle of blessings and those blessings should flow to people around you.

So when God wants to pour you an oversize blessing He doesn't look at you alone, he looks at the 'they' around you. The 'they' people are the ones that will help you carry the blessings. God considers the capacity of your team when he wants to pour his blessing. As much as He wants to bless you, he doesn't want you to sink.

Look around you and see the right people God has provided to help you carry what He wants to give you. Moses had Aaron his brother, Miriam his sister, and the 70 elders of Israel to help him lead a new nation. Gideon had his three hundred warriors that helped him carry the victory God gave him over the Midianites. King David had his mighty men of valor that help him carry the kingdom God gave him. Jesus had his twelve apostles that helped him carry on His huge mission on earth. Simeon had James and John as his fishing partners. There are people God has provided to help you carry the oversize blessings He is releasing to you. It may be a team of people who understands your vision and mission. It may be an organization or corporation that specializes in the field of your endeavor. The truth is that you need the fact that you help to carry the great thing God has sent your way. Some ideas or visions God has given you are bigger to you and if you don't add ships to yours you will sink.

God wants to move you from the local level to the global level. He wants to move you from zero to hero, from obscurity to a celebrity, from no influence to affluence. He wants to move you from working in a company to owning your own company, from being an employee to an employer, from driving the tractor to being the project contractor, from mowing in a field to owning the field. But can you carry it?

God doesn't want to bless you so much that it sinks you. He doesn't want to give you a contract or job that sinks your relationship with your family. He doesn't want to bless you to the level that your fame becomes bait to your Christian faith. To the level that you become too fat that you lack a humble heart. He doesn't want to lift you to a height too high that you can't get on your knees for prayers, that you become too occupied that you can't sit down and listen to His word. He doesn't want to give you a huge success that will drown you. So He wants you to employ ships and seek the helping hands of people who will help you carry it because His plan for you is beyond you alone.

THE LORDS DOING

When Simon Peter saw it, he fell down at Jesus knees, saying, Depart from me; for I am a sinful man, O Lord. For he was astonished, and all that were with him, at the draught of the fishes which they had taken. **(Luke 5:8-9)**

When Simon and his partners saw the miracle he knew that was the Lords doing and it was marvelous in their sight. They got in ten minutes what they never got in ten years and that could only be God. Not their skills, not their talents, not their years of experience but God. Only God could do that. They were like them that dream dreams when God turned back the captivity of Zion (Psalm126:1).

God wants to do something in your life that you will say – Nobody else but You Lord. He will do something that you will acknowledge that it is not your university degrees that got it for you, not your years of experience, not that you are the best in what you do, not your everyday hustle, not that you are very smart with a high IQ better than Albert Einstein, not that you are prettier than Miss World, not that you have connections in high places, not that you are as rich as Jeff Bezos, it is God.

He will do something that will make you realize that indeed the race is not for the swift, the battle is not for the strong, the bread is not for the wise, riches are not for the men of understanding and favor is not for men of skills. You will see that it is not him that "*...willeth, nor of him that runneth but of God that sheweth mercy.*" **(Romans 9:16).**You will thank Him that He decided to show you mercy. He indeed shows mercy to whom He wants to show mercy and compassion to the one He chooses **(Romans 9:15).**

Nobody knew that in the mind of Simon, the young preacher Jesus was another charlatan that was deceiving the mass. He believed the messiah would not come from Nazareth. Even if the messiah came from there by mistake it wouldn't be this used-to-be carpenter that developed magical powers overnight. He didn't attend the crusade because he saw people who did as lazy folks. He said Christianity was a scam and preachers were businessmen like him. He didn't believe in miracles. Even when he heard of the miracles Jesus did, he said it was staged because such things were impossible. He said people were being hypnotized in Jesus' ministry. He was among the free thinkers who didn't want to do anything with religion because it is called the opium of the mass. Despite that, the Lord showed him mercy.

When Simon realized that the Lord showed him mercy he went on his knees because he founded what a great sinner he had been by ignoring Jesus and calling him names. He has been selfish and self-centered all his life; everything was all about him that he gave no thoughts to God. He had negligence for the word of God where his miracles lay. He was not suffering because he was under a curse. He was suffering because he stood away from the One who could change his destiny. Simon discovered that he was unworthy yet Jesus chose to bless him.

AT HIS FEET

When Simon experienced the huge breakthrough in his fishing business he was supposed to be busy counting his million fishes and come up with new business plans on how to distribute and sell them instead he left them all and fell at the knee of Jesus confessing that he was a sinner. Simon realized that being busy with business while ignoring the Lord achieved nothing for him.

Have you realized the reason you suffered what you suffered? Have you seen the reason you are a great person groping your way through life, gambling on things to find where you belong? It is not that you were cursed; it was not that you are not good enough not pretty enough, not smart enough. It was because you are avoiding your destiny changer. You are far from the One who is the Author and Finisher of your destiny. You neglect the word that created you and created the earth upon which you live, He created the sea where you fish and the field where you work.

It is time you should go back to His feet and fall on His knees. One morning with the King changes everything. One day, listening to Him can forever change your story. One moment in His presence, you will never be the same. That's where you get a reflection of who are and a revelation of what you are capable of doing and getting. At His feet is where you discover yourself because success and breakthrough in life are more of discovery.

CHAPTER 7

HERE COMES YOUR DESTINY

In John Lanes book title Timeless Simplicity, there is a rich industrialist who was horrified to find a fisherman lying beside his boat, smoking a pipe.

"Why aren't you fishing?" asked the industrialist.

"Because I have caught enough fish for the day."

"Why don't you catch some more?"

"What would I do with them?"

"You could earn more money. Then you could have a motor fitted to your boat to go into deeper waters and catch more fish. Then you would have enough money to buy nylon nets. These would bring you more fish and more money. Soon you would have enough money to own two boats... maybe even a fleet of boats. Then you would be a rich man like me."

"What would I do then?"

"Then you could sit back and enjoy life."

"What do you think I'm doing right now?"

"Some people are like the rich industrialist, their goal in life is to build a business empire, own multimillion-dollar companies, make massive investments, have properties in the exotic parts of the earth then sit back and live like a king. Some people are like the fisherman, they don't want an empire of anything, if they can fry the fish they catch, eat it with their daily bread then they will sit back and smoke their pipe, gaze into the sky, and smile at the moon."

We have different goals and visions in life. What is enough for me may not be enough for you. Where you stopped may be where I choose to start. Some people retire at a certain age where another reaches and chooses to aspire more. Someone's excellence is another's mediocrity. What stops many people in life is not failures, they have handled failures severally, what stops many people is success. Some people didn't wash their net after several attempts to catch something, they washed their net after they caught so much because they felt they don't need to fish again ever in their lives. Every day becomes a party for them because they feel they have enough and they have arrived.

But life is more than sitting back after your success to live like a king. It is more than having a vacation on the Caribbean beach, relaxing on your yacht, and smoking a pipe. Life is more than being named the richest man by Forbes Magazine.

DONT BE A FOOL

This reminds me of a parable Jesus gave about a certain rich man:

"And he spake a parable unto them, saying, The ground of a certain rich man brought forth plentifully: And he thought within himself, saying, what shall I do, because I have no room where to bestow my fruits? And he said, This will I do: I will pull down my barns, and build greater; and there will I bestow all my fruits and my goods. And I will say to my soul, Soul, thou hast much goods laid up for many years; take thine ease, eat, drink, and be merry. But God said unto him, Thou fool, this night thy soul shall be required of thee: then whose shall those things be, which thou hast provided?" **(Luke. 12:16-20)**

I know how you pray for God to give you your own financial breakthrough. I know how you want to get married and have your own children. I know how you want to be a millionaire. I know how big and lofty your dreams are. You know how you have your life well planned and written out.

Many of us lived our lives trying to escape poverty and eventually after they did escape poverty, they had nothing else to live for. They asked for plenty and plenty came and they lose their sense of purpose. Many church folks stopped going to church the moment they got the blessing they were praying for. You get to see a lot of women in prayer meetings asking God for a husband, children, healing, and comfort for their hurt. Then the moment they get those, you become too preoccupied for God. Funny enough, many of us are not prepared for life after a breakthrough.

I won't forget a story a man shared with us about his governor friend. He said that his friend won the governorship election of his state. He went to visit him to congratulate him; on getting to his house he was told that he can't see him. He inquired why they told him that the governor-elect was too drunk to attend to anyone. He had to sleep over to see his friend in the morning at least say congrats and goodbye at the same time. In the morning he met his governor-elect friend who was at the moment sober, he asked him why he got so drunk after winning an election, was it out of celebration and jubilation. His governor friend said No. To his greatest amazement, his governor friend said that he became drunk because he had never in his life been that confused. He said he planned so much to win the election but didn't have a plan to lead his state after the election. What an elected fool!

Many plans so much to succeed but they don't have any other plan after success. They work so much to get money but they don't have any plan for the right use of the money. Their plan has always been all about them. The kind of car to drive, the kind of house to build, the kind of pictures they will post on social media, the glamour of the party they want to host. The only plan some of us have is like the rich industrialist said, *Sit back and enjoy life. Smoke a pipe* and *observe the sunset.* But God doesn't bless anybody for those things. And if you think God is blessing you for any of those things you are thinking like the old rich fool who said, *Soul, thou hast much goods laid up for many years; take thine ease, eat, drink, and be merry.*

God has a better and bigger plan for you than you can ever imagine. He has a better plan for you.

THE GREATEST OF ALL TIME

Though Moses was busy enjoying elegant life as the prince of Egypt yet he wasn't satisfied. He had everything he wanted but deep down inside of him he knew life should be beyond that. Joseph was enjoying the pleasure of being the favorite prince of Jacob but destiny called him out, sent him to Egypt where he was the head slave who lacked nothing in Potiphar's house even when he found himself in the prison dungeon of Egypt he still emerged as the chief prisoner yet his destiny was beyond all that. Daniel was given the privilege to be a president and live the executive life he wanted in the two empires that ruled the ancient world yet he was deeply concerned about the state of Gods people in captivity. Esther became the queen of Persia by miracle, a position no woman of Jewish origin ever attained yet she knew she was there for a purpose. Such a breakthrough can make someone to be carried away with pleasures, but these people I mentioned understood God had a better plan for them more than the great height where they found themselves.

"For brass, I will bring gold, and for iron, I will bring silver, and for wood brass, and for stones iron." **(Isaiah 60:17)**

You may be enjoying wood but God wants to give you stone, you may be enjoying stone but God wants to give you brass, you may be enjoying brass but He wants to give you silver. And you may be enjoying silver that you think you have gotten everything you needed but God wants to give you gold. Don't settle for silver when God is waiting to give you gold. If you think gold is the last thing to get, He has diamonds as well. You may think that Gods plan for you is to make you a millionaire but He wants to make you a billionaire. You may think he only wants to make you great; he wants to make you the greatest of all time.

He made Simon the greatest fisherman of his time by catching that huge number of fishes that filled his ships but He had a bigger better plan for Simon. It was when Simon came close than he used to that he saw the bigger picture. Jesus wanted more than his ship, he wanted the life of Simon, He wanted his time. He wanted Simon to fall at His feet and knee just to know Him the more.

"And Jesus said unto Simon, Fear not; from henceforth thou shalt catch men. And when they had brought their ships to land, they forsook all, and followed him." **(Luke 5:10-11)**

Everything you passed through was equipping and preparing you for destiny. All those things happened for the greater assignment and bigger plans He has for you. Amid your disappointment, failures, frustrations, hardship, heartbreaks, rejections, and setbacks, it was God who was preparing you for where He is taking you. You were in His plan when you were the groping great; you were still in his plan when you failed at your past. He was teaching you patience when you came to the end of the rope. He was teaching you endurance when you couldn't get any catch when your sustenance ran dry and you wanted to give up because you have had enough of the pain.

You may not have become who He destined you to be but you are not who used to be when you started. You may not have reached where He is taking you but you are not where you used to be ten years ago. Your curriculum vitae have improved, your muscles are stronger, your visions are clearer, and your character is more trustworthy. If you could catch fishes, you can catch humans. If you could lead sheep as David did, then you can lead a kingdom. If you could lead a big household like Potiphar's house and take care of prisoners as Joseph did, then you can handle the affairs of a whole empire and continent. If you can handle small things effectively and efficiently, God will commit greater things to you.

God understands that your destiny and purpose lie not in your determination but in your discovery so He put you through some processes for you to discover Him (God) and to discover yourself. He knows that what you love is a clue to the gifts and talents He has given so He allowed you to experiment with your abilities till you develop them. He knows that your grief is a clue to something you are assigned to heal so He let you experience some grieves so that you can understand it better in order to heal others who are grieving. He knows that what you hate is a clue to something you are destined to correct so He lets you experience some things you hated. It was Him working in you to achieve His purpose.

Jesus turned Simon Peter from being a fisherman to become the greatest apostle of all time. Peter may not have written the number of epistles like Paul maybe because he was not as educated (intellectually) as Paul was but to me Peter is the greatest apostle of all time. He didn't give up and Jesus never gave up on him,

Gods plan for you is to make you the greatest of all time in something. It doesn't mean that you will be famous, well known all over the world and very rich. It means being a blessing to your world, your family, your community, and your corporation that they will be very grateful and thankful that you lived. To your children, you may be the greatest father or mother of all time. To your students, you may be the greatest teacher of all time. To your family, you may be the greatest relative of all time. To your organization, you may the greatest member of all time. To your lover, you may be the greatest lover of all time. To your church member, you may be the greatest pastor, preacher, or teacher of all time. To your team, you may be the greatest team player of all time.

Your impact on their life is beyond expression. You are their hero or heroine. Their help in the time of their need. Their comforter when they mourn. Their happiness when life is sad to them. They find hope in your presence and faith in your words. They find love in your touch and solace in your embrace. Like Joseph, you are the one sent ahead to preserve your family and entire race from being consumed by a coming economic meltdown. Like Moses, you are the reason they will not die in slavery. Like Joshua, you are the leader that will lead them to their inheritance. Like Queen Esther, you are the reason your people will not be exterminated.

Your life is far beyond what you think it is. That's why you should never ever, ever, ever give up. Don't wash your net yet because what you think has ended has just begun because God has stepped in. Like a movie with a happy ending keep playing your role according to your script. It will surely end happily ever after if you don't give up.

ABOUT THE AUTHOR

Chidi C. ObiGod is human development and relationship life coach, a motivational speaker, writer, and poet with a degree in Medical physiology. He is passionate about identifying potentials in young people, helping them discover and tap into the greatness that lies in them.

He is the founder of PEP House; a faith-based non-profit organization that aims to give people POWER, inspire them toward EXCELLENCE to fulfill their PURPOSE in life.

CONNECT WITH ME

Follow me on Twitter:@IamtheOne_777

Instagram: chidiobigod

Send me an email: ceceobigod@gmail.com

OTHER BOOKS BY THE AUTHOR

You Can Be What You Want To Be
Destined To Fly
I Have A Dream (Awakening Your Star)
The Beach In My Heart (100 Poem Anthology)
Dangerous Damsels (10 Toxic Women You Should Avoid)
Prince Harming (12 Men That Are Not The One For You)

ABOUT THE BOOK

Have you ever felt tired of life because you don't see a reason to live anymore?

Have you felt like giving up on everybody and everything because of disappointments?

Have you felt like a failure because you are no longer seeing results as you envisioned?

Have you ever contemplated suicide and no one knows about it but you?

Well, you are not the first to pass through that dark tunnel before. Some people have passed through that dark tunnel and they came out with a testimony because they find light in the tunnel.

This book serves as a light to all those going through the dark tunnel of life. Instead of groping in the darkness of depression and uncertainty why not follow the direction of the light this book will give you. By the time you follow the light, you will get in this book, the darkness that makes you depressed will be gone. The darkness that makes you feel like a failure to the extent that you want to wash your career, business, relationship, and the ministerial net will disappear as you begin to see what God has in store for you.

The author used the story of a fisherman named Simon who had a colossal failure before experiencing a titanic success in his fishing business to give you the reasons why you should not give up on what destiny has in store for you.